OOMPH

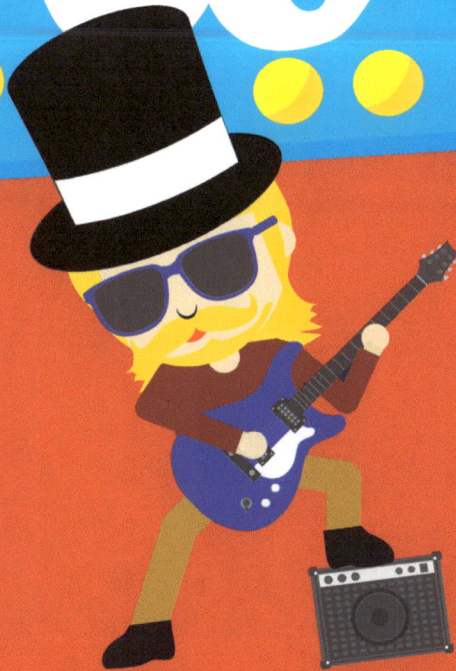

A World of Words

Written by Anne Lingelbach

Illustrated by Kellen Roggenbuck

In Honor of Arty, the Little White Dog

Published by Orange Hat Publishing 2017
ISBN 978-1-948365-04-8

www.orangehatpublishing.com

Welcome to the World of Oomph

This is a place where wondrous words reside. It is where writers go when they are looking for unusual words which will add pizzazz or oomph to their writing.

These words are weird, wacky, and fun to say.

Quaff (quaf) – to drink quickly: The sports player quaffed the sports drink after the game.

Doozy (do-zee) – something extraordinary: The three pointer that ended the basketball game was a real doozy!

Barla-fumble (bar-luh-fum-ble) – a call for a time-out: The basketball coach called a barla-fumble after the missed play.

Oxter (ahks-ter) – an armpit: After the basketball game, the players had sweaty oxters.

Lickety-split (lick-e-tee-split) – as fast as possible: The basketball player ran lickety-split around the court to block the ball against the opposing team.

Gussy (guh-see) — to dress up: The girl was gussied up in her best clothes to go to the birthday party.

Biffy (bif-ee) — a toilet: Our huge dog likes to drink water out of the biffy.

Fernticle (fern-tik-le) — a freckle: My big sister has many fernticles on her face.

Bumf (bumfh) — toilet paper: My little sister pretends that she is a puppy when she grabs the end of the bumf and runs around.

no drinking

Scamander (skuh-mand-er) — to wander about: The lost child scamandered in the forest.

Gallinipper (gal-i-nip-er) — a large mosquito: My parents use bug spray to keep the gallinippers away from us when we play outside.

Vug (vuhg) – a cave: The brown bear just emerged from her vug.

Ramshackle (ram-shak-le) – badly constructed, ready to fall apart: The ramshackle cottage was very old.

Itty-bitty (i-tee-bi-tee) – very small: The itty-bitty ladybug landed on the grass.

Hoddy-noddy (ha-dee-nod-dee) – a foolish person: The castle's hoddy-noddy is scheduled to perform for the princess.

Skedaddle (ski-dad-le) – to hurry somewhere: The white mouse skedaddled away from the tabby cat.

Booffage (boo-fahzh) – a filling meal: A holiday meal is certainly a booffage because no one is hungry after eating it.

Cosher (kahsh-er) – to feast: The princess and her guests were coshering at the banquet.

Festoon (fest-oon) – to decorate: The Great Hall was festooned with birthday balloons.

Knabble (nab-le) – to nibble: The white mouse knabbled on the piece of cheese.

Burgoo (burr-goo) – a stew or thick soup: In the winter, many people enjoy eating burgoo with a baguette.

Dollop (doll-up) – a small amount of a soft substance: There was a dollop of whipped cream on top of the ice cream sundae.

Pluteus (ploo-tee-uhs) – a bookshelf: The classroom pluteus was filled with amazing books.

Holus-bolus (ho-lus-bo-lus) – all at once: The marbles scattered holus-bolus onto the floor.

Hiccius doccius (hick-shee-us dock-shee-us) – abracadabra: The magician left his hat and wand in the classroom after saying his final hiccius doccius.

Gilly-gaupus (gil-ee-gaw-pus) – a silly person: His behavior was so funny that people called him a gilly-gaupus.

Ebullient (i-byoo-lient) – enthusiastic: The student was ebullient about participating in the spelling bee.

Badot (bad-doh) – silly: Badot behavior can cause problems in the classroom.

Rataplan (rat-uh-plan) – to beat a drum: The percussionist rataplanned the drum loudly.

Collywobbles (kol-lee-wob-bles) – butterflies in the stomach: The band members had collywobbles because it was their first concert.

Magnolious (mag-noh-lee-us) – great, large, magnificent: The applause gave the musicians a magnolious feeling.

Choler (kah-ler) – a double chin: The dog's collar was tight because it had a choler.

Honeyfuggle (huh-nee-fuh-guhl) – to cheat or trick: The man wanted to win the card game so he honeyfuggled.

Snollygoster (sno-lee-go-ster) – a person who can't be trusted: A person who cheats at games is a snollygoster.

Befuddled (be-fudd-ld) – confused: The befuddled player didn't understand the directions for the board game.

Pilliver (pi-li-ver) – a pillowcase:
Some kids use pillivers for candy
bags on Halloween.

Curwhibble (kur-whib-ble) – a thingamagig, a
whatchamacallit: The small child did not know
the correct name for the curwhibble.

Obambulate (ob–am–byoo–late) – to wander about: The ghosts obambulated throughout the haunted house.

Gangrel (gang-grul) – a child beginning to walk: The parents were so proud of their gangrel that they took several pictures to share with family members.

Whelve (whelv) – to bury something: The pirates whelved the treasure chest in a remote part of the island.

Taradiddle (tar-uh-di-dle) – a lie: The fisherman's story about how he caught the fish was a huge taradiddle.

Youf (yowf) – a muffled bark: The elderly dog's youf caught the attention of his owner.

Hubbub (hub-bub) – loud noise: The colorful fireworks caused a hubbub on the 4th of July.

Spawl (spawl) – to spit: The boy was spawling cherry pits on the ground.

Finicky (fin-ik-kee) – very particular about what you want: My little brother does not like to eat foods that are squishy; Mom says that he's a finicky eater.

Viduous (vid-yoo-uhs) – empty: The child was upset when he discovered that his piggy bank was viduous.

Rapscallion (rap-scal-li-on) – a rascal: The rapscallion ate most of the cookies in the cookie jar.

Skosh (skosh) – a small amount of something: I put a skosh of whipped cream in my steaming mug of hot chocolate.

Futz (futz) – to waste time: The students had homework because they futzed around during work time.

Hodgepodge (hodge-podge): a random mixture of items: We have a junk drawer in our kitchen that has a hodgepodge of things in it.

dfhsgh!

COOKIES

Gobbledygook (gob-ble-dee-gook) – words that don't make sense: My baby brother speaks gobbledygook.

Nidify (ni-di-fie) – to build a nest: The bluebird nidified a home for her eggs.

Phoenicurous (fen-i-kyoor-us) – red-tailed: The phoenicurous hawk flew low in the sky looking for food.

Emydosaurian (e-mi-do-saw-ree-uhn) – a crocodile: The teeth of the emydosaurian look terrifying.

Aucupate (aw-kyoo-pate) – to go bird watching: The scientist was aucupating for bald eagles in the sky.

Bicrural (bye-kroor-uhl) – two-legged: The bicrural bird sat on the window sill.

Flaffer (flaff-er) – to flutter: The tiny red bird flaffered around the bird feeder.

Tellurian (tuh-loo-ree-uhn) – an inhabitant of the earth: We are all earthlings or tellurians.

Otacust (oh-tuh-kust) – an eavesdropper or spy: The otacust took pictures of the secret information.

Glom (glom) –
to steal: The
thief glommed
money from the
convenience
store.

Gewgaw (gew-gaw) – a trinket that
is not worth much: The woman bought
several gewgaws at the rummage sale.

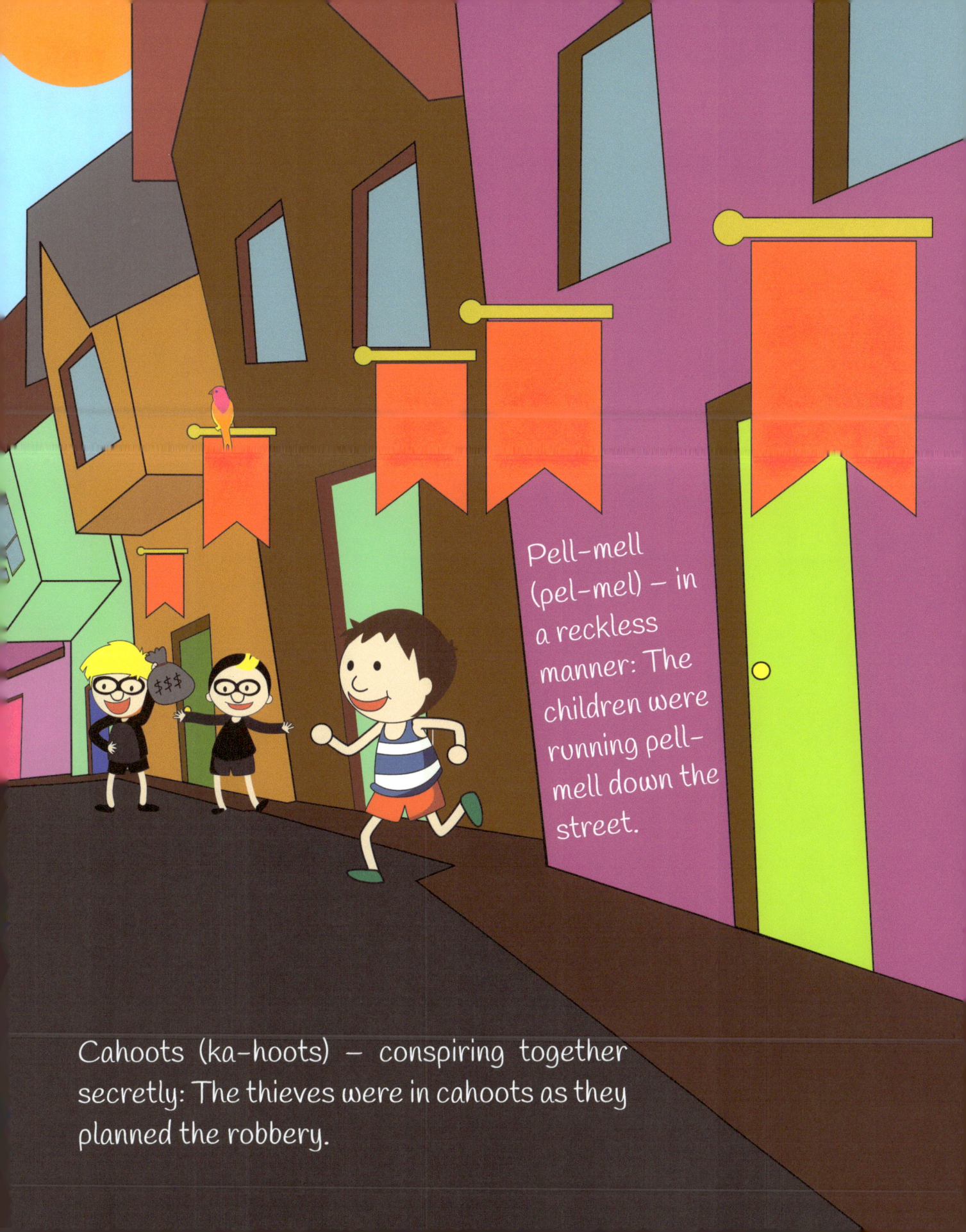

Pell-mell (pel-mel) – in a reckless manner: The children were running pell-mell down the street.

Cahoots (ka-hoots) – conspiring together secretly: The thieves were in cahoots as they planned the robbery.

Turngiddy – dizzy from spinning around: The child felt turngiddy after spinning around on the merry-go-round.

Argle-bargle – a loud quarrel: The little kids had an argle-bargle at recess.

Shenanigan – a prank: These kids are always pulling shenanigans on their teacher.

Lollygag – to fall behind: The girl lollygagged behind the rest of the class.

Hither – to this place: "Come hither," the teacher said as she gestured to the classroom door.

www.ingramcontent.com/pod-product-compliance
Lightning Source LLC
LaVergne TN
LVHW072133070426
835513LV00002B/83